By:

Judith M. Singley

Trees are terrific...
Judy Singley
2012

Written with Love for Adalynn, Carson, Joshua, and Lucas

All of the photographs in this book were taken in Cass County Michigan. None of them have been altered except to crop the image for a closer view. A special thank you to Larry and Alma McClelland for allowing us to walk in their beautiful woods where some of the photos were taken. All of the pictures were taken in October to showcase Michigan's autumn foliage.

Order this book online at www.trafford.com
or email orders@trafford.com

Most Trafford titles are also available at major online book retailers.

Printed in the United States of America.

ISBN: 978-1-4669-4640-8

Library of Congress Control Number: 2012911966

Trafford rev. 08/22/2012

Trafford
PUBLISHING   www.trafford.com

North America & international
toll-free: 1 888 232 4444 (USA & Canada)
phone: 250 383 6864 ◆ fax: 812 355 4082

How to use this book

PARENTS

This book is meant to grow with your child. Young children will enjoy looking at the pictures and hearing the rhymes. Children with letter recognition will want to find the letter shapes in the trees and trace them with their fingers. As they grow and become curious about the outdoors and trees, they will learn from the factual paragraphs.

TEACHERS

Younger children will enjoy seeing the pictures and hearing the rhymes. You may want to chant the rhymes and come up with actions that go with the poems: pantomime planting trees and then sway in the breeze. Letters can be made out of twigs for tactile learners. Take a nature walk to look for more shapes in trees. Make a seasonal tree scrapbook and celebrate Arbor Day and Earth Day by planting trees.

Older children may use the book for reading practice and as a trade book in science class. They may want to write their own nature poems, collect leaves in the fall and buds in the spring. Do leaf and bark rubbings. Projects could include drawing and labeling cross sections of trees, researching and reporting how the school could be more environmentally responsible, compiling an identification booklet for trees around the school, and sponsoring an Arbor Day and Earth Day celebration.

No matter what the age of the reader, the book is meant to celebrate trees and foster appreciation for the wonders found in nature.

Aa

A is for Arbor Day
planting new trees,

A rbor Day was started by J. Sterling Morton. He was a journalist from Detroit, Michigan. After becoming Secretary of the Nebraska Territory, he wanted to spread the word about the importance of trees. On April 10, 1872, Nebraska celebrated the first Arbor Day by planting a million trees. Today Arbor Day is celebrated at different times worldwide.

B is for branches
that sway in the breeze.

B ranches are to trees as arms are to humans. Humans only have two, but a tree can have many. Branches grow out of the tree's trunk. Large branches are sometimes called limbs or boughs. Small ones are called twigs. Bark covers the branches and helps protect the inner parts of the tree.

C is for cones
some are long some are round,

Conifer means having cones. The most common conifer tree is the pine. Pine trees have needle-shaped leaves and cones. The needle bundles and cones help identify the type of pine. White pines have five needles per bundle, and their cones are long and thin. Jack pines only have two needles per bundle, and their cones are small and round with a curve at one end.

D is for dropping
their leaves to the ground.

Deciduous means to "fall off", so trees that lose their leaves for part of the year are deciduous. Trees make their own food called chlorophyll. Chlorophyll is what makes leaves green. When days get shorter and the weather turns cooler, trees stop making their food and the green color changes. A leaf's natural color is the red, yellow, orange, or brown you see in autumn.

E is for evergreen
spruce, fir and pine,

E vergreen trees stay green all year. These trees may shed some needles or leaves but not all at once. Most evergreens are conifers having needles. Tropical trees are known as broadleaf evergreens that keep their leaves all year.

F is for forest by nature's design.

Forests are areas of land covered by trees and underbrush. They cover about 30% of the Earth's surface. There are many different types of forests. Boreal forests are in cold places. Temperate zones or places with a milder climate have broadleaf deciduous and evergreen coniferous trees. Tropical jungles are known as rainforests and grow close to the equator where it is hot.

Gg

G is for green
conservation is good,

G oing "green" means to be more responsible for protecting and preserving Earth's environment. One way to help the environment is to recycle or reuse products instead of throwing them away to fill up the landfills. Using solar and wind power also helps protect the environment from pollution. More and more businesses are being developed to help people repair and restore Earth's atmosphere.

H is for homes
that are built out of wood.

Homes are built of wood. This type of wood is called lumber. Lumber is used to make a sturdy frame for the shape of the house. After the house is framed-in, walls and a roof are put on it. The outside of the house can be wood shingles, although some homes are covered with vinyl siding or brick. Homes are filled with furniture, also made from wood.

I is for important
a lasting effect,

Important means having great value and that defines trees. Trees help to clean our air supply by changing carbon dioxide into oxygen. They provide food and shelter for people, animals, birds, and insects. Tree roots hold the soil in place to prevent erosion. Trees planted close to homes can add value by helping to cool them in the summer and protect them in the winter. Trees also make the world a beautiful place.

J is for jungles
we need to protect.

Jungles are very dense and provide homes to many different plants and animals. Jungles are made up of shrubs, vines, and small trees. They grow on the edge of the much taller rainforests. About 6% of the Earth's land mass consists of jungles and rainforests, and over 50% of all plant and animal species on Earth live there. Jungles provide food, wood, and medicines to the world.

K is for kindling
a cozy campfire,

Kindling consists of small dry sticks used to start a fire. Campfires are usually built in a fire ring using sand or dirt as the base. The circle can be made from small rocks. A fire ring should not be too close to trees, overhead branches, or anything flammable. Kindling catches fire quickly. As it burns, larger pieces of dry wood can be added. It is fun to camp out and roast hot dogs and marshmallows around a cozy campfire.

L is for limbs
holding leaves that transpire.

Leaves transpire, or release water vapor into the air. Transpiration in trees is a little bit like sweating in humans. When people get too warm, they perspire to cool down. Leaves do the same. On really hot days a tree can lose gallons of water. Trees in very hot climates have thicker, smaller leaves or needles so they lose less water when they "sweat".

M is for maple sap syrupy sweet,

Maple syrup is made from the sap of maple trees. Sap is a liquid found in trees and is made of water, sugars, and nutrients that trees need. As spring begins and the weather starts to warm up, sap stored in a tree's roots begins to flow up into the branches. Native Americans discovered that if they collected and heated this sap, it turned into a sweet tasty food.

N is for nature
the world's heartbeat.

Nature means the outside world and everything that lives there. Food, shelter, air, and water are all given by nature. People depend on nature for survival and it is important to keep nature in balance. Nature is the world's heartbeat; we need to keep it healthy.

O is for oxygen
trees freshen the air,

Oxygen is given off by trees during photosynthesis. Photosynthesis is how plants make their own food. Green trees, algae, and shrubs absorb carbon dioxide and water and use the energy of the sun to change them into chlorophyll food. Oxygen is given off as a waste product during this process. Humans and animals use oxygen to breathe in and fuel their body, and then they give carbon dioxide back to the trees.

P is for planting
more trees everywhere.

Planting trees is not only fun, but helpful to our world. Trees are pretty easy to plant. They can be started from seeds and transplanted when they get large enough, or they can be bought from tree farms or greenhouses. Make sure to give young trees plenty of water during hot, dry weather.

Q is for quiet
enjoy the outdoors,

Quiet and calm is definitely what you will get when you walk in the woods. Nature has her own language and it includes the sound of breezes through leaves, the rustle of animals and birds among the dry underbrush, and the crunch of twigs as you walk. Foreign languages may be difficult to learn but everyone understands the quiet of nature's language.

R is for resource renews and restores.

Resources can be renewable or nonrenewable. An example of a nonrenewable resource is copper. Once all the copper is mined, it will be gone forever. Then the only supply will be whatever can be recycled. Lucky for us, trees are a renewable resource. Renewable resources are ones that can be re-grown over and over. Most trees grow slowly so it is important to replace the ones that have fallen or been cut down.

S is for shade
to get out of the sun,

S hade trees are usually ones that grow large with spreading limbs to cast a big shadow. Maples and oaks make good shade trees. Public parks use trees to shade playgrounds and walking trails. It is nice to relax under the protection of a tree and cool down in its shadow.

T is for treehouse and summertime fun.

Treehouses can be small and simple or large and fancy. Small ones are usually a platform built on the first strong limb of a tree. It can be a fun neighborhood clubhouse or just a place to read a good book. Large treehouses are sometimes built as a tourist attraction. Crossville, Tennessee, has a large treehouse built around a huge oak tree. Horace Burgess built it ten stories high out of donated recycled wood.

U is for underbrush hiding wildlife,

Underbrush means small trees or a thicket of shrubs growing under larger trees in the forest. It provides shelter and food for animals and birds. It also covers fallen leaves and branches that blanket the forest floor. The underbrush provides a dark, damp place just right for plant decay. Plant and animal decomposition helps to make the soil rich and fertile.

V is for value
trees add to our life.

"Value Trees" would make a great motto. Trees not only help clean the air, prevent soil erosion, and produce building materials, but they also supply a great variety of food. Fruits, nuts, chocolate, coffee, and even root beer come from trees. Tree bark, leaves, flowers, and roots also provide valuable medicines.

W is for wood
to be sculpted and hewed,

Wood is unique. It is easy to work with and has many uses. Wood chips can be used for mulch in gardens or ground into pulp for making paper. Wood makes solid floors, doors, furniture, boats, and structures. It can be sculpted into pieces of art. It is used for fuel to heat homes and for flavors in smoking foods.

X is for xylem
that carries tree food.

Xylem is a vital part of wood. Together with phloem it carries water and nutrients to all the parts of a tree from roots to leaves. Xylem and phloem can be compared to veins and arteries. In humans, veins and arteries carry blood, oxygen, and nutrients to the body's cells. In trees the same function is performed by xylem and phloem. The phloem is right next to the bark; the xylem is in the next layer of wood.

Y is for you
to appreciate their worth,

You are just as important to trees as they are to you because you can help to protect and preserve them. The most important way to do that is to become educated in ways to practice conservation. People need trees for food, shelter, and jobs. Trees need people to plant and reforest the Earth.

Z is for zest
to reforest the Earth.

Zest is another word for enthusiasm. If there is one thing to be enthusiastic about it is trees. Knowing how important they are is the first step in appreciating our environment. Everyone can help to reforest the Earth. So, on the next Arbor Day, grab your shovel and zestfully plant some trees.

Glossary

C

<u>Canopy</u> – the top or uppermost spreading layer of a forest

<u>Carbon dioxide</u> – a colorless gas exhaled by animals and humans and absorbed by plants during photosynthesis

<u>Chlorophyll</u> – the green coloring matter of plants

<u>Coniferous</u> – trees and shrubs that have cones

<u>Conservation</u> – careful preservation and protection of natural resources to prevent pollution or neglect

D

<u>Deciduous</u> – falling off at the end of a season

<u>Decompose (decomposition)</u> – to rot, or break down into different parts

E

<u>Embers</u> – a glowing piece of wood or ash

<u>Environment</u> – surroundings that affect living things

<u>Erosion</u> – to wear away by water, wind, or ice

H

<u>Habitat</u> – the place where plants or animals naturally grow with all they need

<u>Hew (hewed)</u> – to carve or shape wood

J

<u>Journalist</u> – a writer for a newspaper or magazine

M

<u>Motto</u> – an expression that guides conduct

N

<u>Nonrenewable</u> – not able to be replaced like oil, coal, minerals, gems

<u>Nutrient</u> – to give nourishment

P

Phloem – a series of tubes in trees and plants that carry water and

nutrients

Photosynthesis – plant's ability to make their own food

Pollution – to make impure, to spoil a resource like air, water, land.

R

Recycle – to use again as in glass, plastic, aluminum

Renewable – able to be replaced or regrown

S

Solar power – using the energy from the sun to create power

T

Transpire (transpiration) – plants that give off water vapor

W

Wind power – using the energy of wind to create power

X

Xylem – the part of a plant that carries water and nutrients